Laurindo Almeida

Contemporary Moods for Classical Guitar

© Copyright 1970

ROBBINS MUSIC CORPORATION
NEW YORK, N.Y.

Laurindo Almeida

Laurindo Almeida is the complete musician. One of the world's several truly great concert guitarists, he is ever being compared to Segovia, whom he knows and respects. In the past year he has played dozens of concerts, performing the works of the masters. Yet recently he toured much of the world as featured soloist with the Modern Jazz Quartet.

He brought Bossa Nova to the U.S. long before it was called that; he has scored many films, often composing, then playing his own music; and his famed recordings include everything from Bach to a beautiful solo album of Broadway favorites. Each of these things he has done superbly, for he is unique among guitarists, and is so acclaimed by audiences and critics alike.

Almeida was born in Sao Paulo, Brazil, on September 2, 1917. He received his earliest musical training from his mother, a concert pianist, who had chosen her own instrument for her son. His sister Maria was the guitar student, but it was Laurindo instead who mastered and fell in love with it.

It soon became evident that when Laurindo played guitar, others loved it as much as he did. This led to concerts in his home city, then in Rio de Janeiro, where his fame began to spread.

In 1936, the youthful Almeida signed as a musician aboard the Brazilian liner Cuyaba, playing, but also listening, learning and absorbing what much of Europe had to offer. Paris gave him his first real taste of jazz, for it was there that he first heard the legendary Django Reinhart with the Hot Club of France.

When he returned to Brazil, Almeida settled in Rio, determined to devote his life to his instrument. He secured a job with Radio Mayrink Veiga and soon became a staff arranger.

By 1944, Laurindo Almeida had become one of Brazil's most famous musicians, admired, even then, by every kind of audience. That year he met Maria Ferreira, a native of Portugal, who had come to Brazil as a dancer. The two were married and, in 1947, moved to the United States.

Coming to Hollywood, he worked for a while in films, and as a concert soloist with violinist Elizabeth Waldo. Then his interest in the things that were happening in American jazz led him to Stan Kenton and a new career.

The Kenton orchestra, always famous for its innovations, gained quickly and handsomely by a kind of guitar music it had never heard before—a cool, quiet sound, spectacular in its brilliance. Famed Kenton arranger Pete Rugolo composed "Lament" to feature Laurindo, and the orchestra accompanied the new star in a concert at the Chicago Opera House before an audience of 20,000. Next it was Almeida's own composition "Amazonia" that was featured at Carnegie Hall, and by year's end, the new arrival had placed third in Down Beat Magazine's annual jazz poll. Now, two decades later, the world's jazz and popular guitarists are still influenced by the things he introduced in those Kenton years.

In 1950, Laurindo Almeida left Kenton to play concerts, to record and to compose; he has now written more than 200 compositions. This was the beginning of yet another career, for through his early classical recordings for Capitol and Decca his fame as a concert artist began to spread, first in the U.S., then in other countries. Many of his concert tours brought new concert forms to people who cheered them then, and warmly remember them now—the beautiful duets with soprano Salli Terri, the Baroque music, his matchless interpretations for lute, the bossa nova he took to Australia and New Zealand along with the Bach and the Renaissance music. In 1966, he performed two American debut recordings of works by two of Brazil's greatest composers: Radames Gnatalli's Concerto de Copacabana and the Villa-Lobos Guitar Concerto.

Today the Almeidas make their home in Sherman Oaks, California. Theirs is a beautiful house with bold, Brazilian interiors, two French Poodles and a rich garden. Long citizens of the U.S., they still see much of the world, for concert demands come from everywhere.

But there is plenty of work for Laurindo Almeida close to home—the nearby Hollywood Bowl; the network television studios, where he may appear as a guest artist or writer-performer for a dramatic show. Here too are most of the major film studios, where Laurindo is composing and playing much of the time.

And here also are other things he enjoys . . . a 28-piece collection of string instruments, which includes his valuable "working guitar," made by Ramerez of Spain, and the mate to Segovia's . . . the collection of fine wines ("but I like to travel, too," he says. "Then I sample the wines wherever I go and bring home the ones I like best") . . . and the pool where he swims each day of the year, as has been his custom since boyhood days, where the beaches at Ipanema and the Copacabana did not require a heater.

Life is very busy for the Almeidas. Busy, but very good . . . as it should be for people who have the taste to live in such a rare aura of success with unaffected grace.

CONTENTS

Book Design: David L'Heureux
Illustrations: Remo Bramanti
Guitar Instruction: Myrna Sislen

THE CONCERT GUITAR

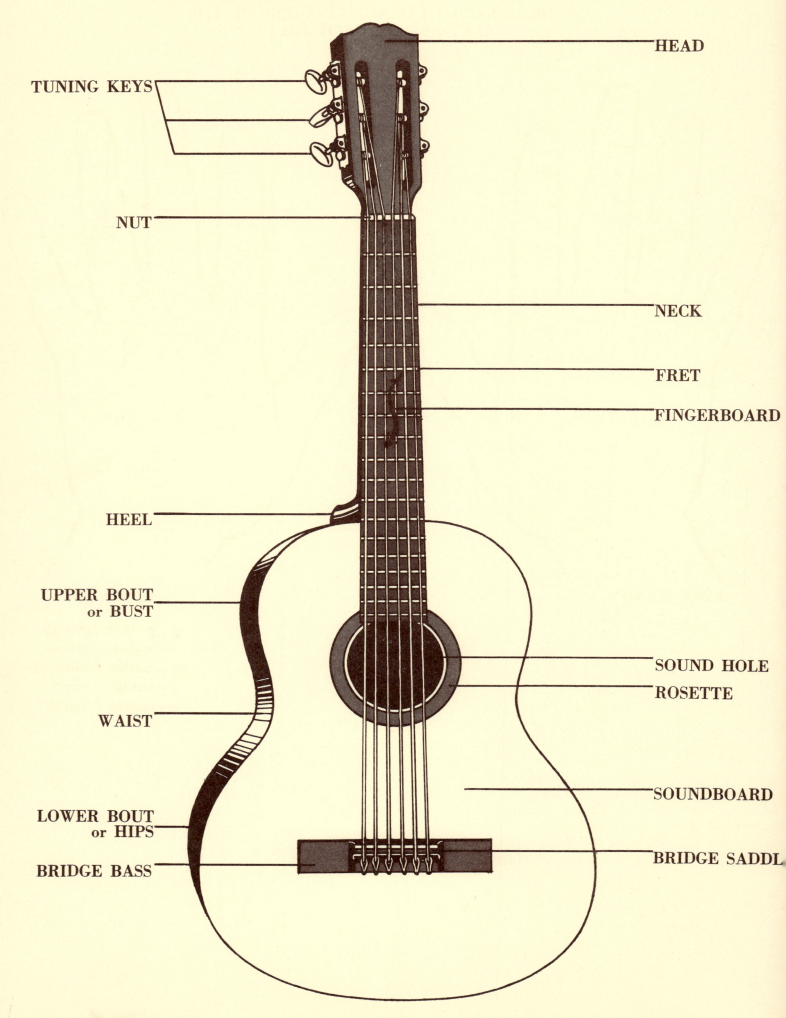

TUNING KEYS

NUT

HEEL

UPPER BOUT
or BUST

WAIST

LOWER BOUT
or HIPS

BRIDGE BASS

HEAD

NECK

FRET

FINGERBOARD

SOUND HOLE

ROSETTE

SOUNDBOARD

BRIDGE SADDL

SYMBOLS USED TO DENOTE FINGERS OF THE
LEFT AND RIGHT HAND

LEFT HAND

RIGHT HAND

p=pulgar *(thumb)*
i=indice *(index)*
m=medio *(middle)*
a=anular *(ring)*
c=cuarto *(fourth)*

HOW TO SIT:

The student should sit on a straight backed chair, with the left foot resting on a stool approximately six to eigh inches in height (individual differences will dictate the need for a higher or lower stool). The right foot should res firmly on the floor. The guitar should be placed on the left thigh so that it is balanced and need not be restrained b either hand. The "head" of the guitar should be parallel with the left shoulder. This position is very important be cause it insures that the instrument will be perfectly balanced and the hands will be free to play. Both male and femal students use the same sitting position, but females should wear culottes or a long skirt to make this position practicable

FIGURE 1

FIGURE 2

RIGHT HAND POSITIONING:

To attain a proper right hand position, keep the guitar properly balanced and rest the elbow on the lower bout of the instrument. Then bring your right hand down until it is hanging freely in front of the sound hole.

The next step is to insure correct positioning for the right hand fingers. First, put the *i, m, a* fingers together and place them on the third string, slightly back from the sound hole *(fig. 1)*. Keeping your fingers in place, put the thumb *(p)* on the second string *(fig. 2)*. Now, without moving your hand take your thumb and place it on the fifth string. The result is that the right hand fingers and thumb are in the shape of an X with the thumb in front and the fingers tilted behind. Now, place the *m* finger on the second string and the *a* finger on the first string and the basic right hand position is complete *(fig. 3 & 4)*. Be

careful while you are playing so as not to let the thumb creep back and get behind the fingers. Also be sure that the right wrist remains slightly arched and that no part of the right hand rests on the guitar.

Keeping this position in mind, there are two ways of striking the strings. The first is called *tirando* or free stroke and is executed by brushing the string in the shape of a shallow arc without touching the next string *(fig. 5)*. *Tirando* is used for fast scale passages or arpeggios. The second stroke is called *apoyando* or rest stroke and is executed by brushing the fingers across one string and coming to rest on the next *(fig. 6)*. *Apoyando* is the stronger stroke and is used to bring out melody lines.

So, now that the right hand position is secure and remembering that the right hand has two ways of striking the strings, *apoyando and tirando*, it is time to add the left hand.

FIGURE 3

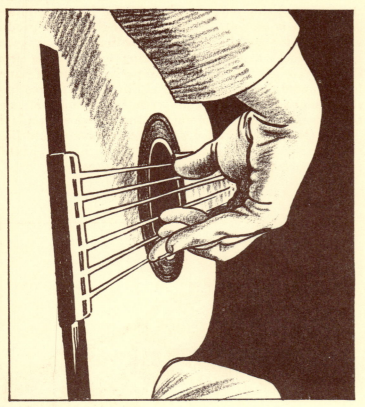

FIGURE 4

FIGURE 5

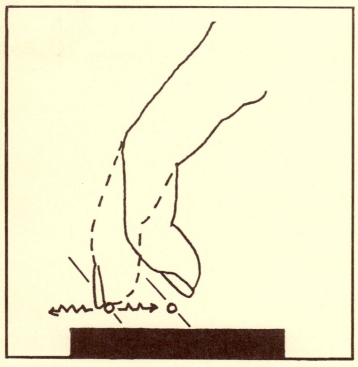

FIGURE 6

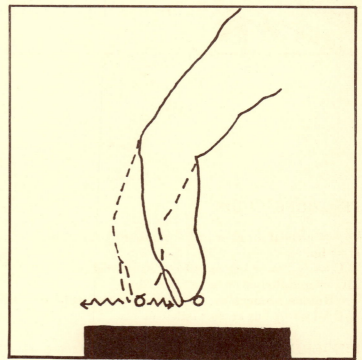

LEFT HAND POSITIONING:

The left hand should play no part in supporting the instrument and is merely used for fingering the notes. This is done by placing the fingers slightly above the desired frets and applying pressure *(fig. 7)*. This pressure is countered by the thumbs, which should be placed somewhat below the middle of the back of the neck *(fig 8)*. Remember, nothing touches the neck of the guitar but the thumb and fingers. If the rest of the hand is allowed to

"hug" the neck, both your speed and clearness of tone will be greatly hampered.

The fingers should naturally fall to four frets with the first finger on the first fret, the second finger on the second fret, the third finger on the third fret and the fourth finger on the fourth fret. This will establish a position that can be moved up the neck of the guitar. It is also important to keep the left hand fingers as close to the strings as possible. If the fingers wander away from the strings, they must be brought back since this increases the chance of missing notes and playing inaccurately. Another point to remember is that the notes should be fingered with just the tip of the left hand fingers. This is accomplished by arching the first little joint upwards. When the tip of the finger is not arched, the finger will touch the adjacent strings and keep them from sounding.

A word should be said about the care and use of fingernails. The left hand nails must be filed very short to accommodate the arching of the fingers that is so necessary for playing. There are many different theories about the most effective way to use the right hand nails. Generally speaking the nails should be rounded to follow the contour of the fingers. These nails are used to re-enforce and give strength to the sound as you strike the strings. Using only the flesh of the finger produces a sound that is too soft, while just using the nail produces one that is too metallic. The combination of the finger and nail produces a good, clear, string tone that is greatly desired. To help file the nails properly, Laurindo Almeida has invented the "Guitarist Level-File". This device fits on the strings and allows the player to file his nails at exactly the same angle that he or she hits the strings when playing. The angle is then rounded with an emery board and finally smoothed with emery paper. The "Guitarist Level-File" is the most accurate way to file the nails properly.

FIGURE 7

FIGURE 8

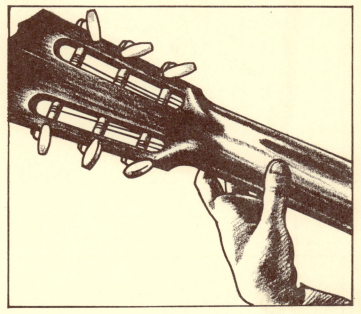

FINGERING GUIDE:

 ② = circled number is the number of the string
C = bar
½C = ½ bar or bar only first three strings
MC = middle bar or bar only middle
V = Roman numeral is the number of the fret for position or bar
½C VI = ½ bar at the sixth fret

FINGERING NOTES :

Arabic numbers printed to the left of the note refer to the fingers of the left hand.

NOTES ABOUT MYRNA SISLEN

Myrna Sislen is a young, talented guitarist and teacher from Washington, D.C. She has studied exclusively with Charlie Byrd, who in turn introduced her to Laurindo Almeida. She has worked closely with Mr. Almeida on a number of musical projects for the past several years. At present, Miss Sislen is teaching with Sophocles Papas in Washington, D.C.

BLUE MOON

LORENZ HART
RICHARD RODGERS

This is a very beautiful straight-forward arrangement and should cause no particular difficulty. However, there are a few places where extra care should be taken.

First of all, be sure to barre VII on the third beat of the 4th measure.

In measure 6, the wavy line in front of the chord, on the fourth beat, indicates that the chord should be arpeggiated or rolled. Other chords are arpeggiated in the arrangement as marked.

The best way to play the third beat of measure 21, is to keep your 4th finger on the G♯ while you are moving from a barre II to a barre I. Measure 25 uses much the same technique. This time keep all your fingers down from the first to the second beat. Only the 2nd finger moves, from A♯ to B♯.

Finally, in measure 32, be sure and barre II on the first beat of the measure.

molto rall.

From the Michael Cacoyannis Production "ZORBA THE GREEK." An International Classics Presentation.

THEME FROM "ZORBA THE GREEK"

MIKIS THEODORAKIS

A circled number ② indicates the string on which a note should be played. In this arrangement, you are told to play the first D♯ on the second string ②. Since both D♯ and B♯ are on the same string, it becomes necessary to play the lower note (B♯) on the next lower string ③. These two notes are then moved up one-half step to E and C♯, with the E played on the second string ②. Much of "Zorba" is made up of these sliding thirds.

In the section beginning with measure 16, the thirds are to be played as grace notes. To achieve this effect, the bass note A should be struck at the same time as the grace notes B♯ and G♯. Remember, grace notes are not counted by themselves. They merely borrow time from the adjacent notes.

The left hand fingering of measure 16 permits the use of a 3/4 bar on the first fret and sliding the bar to the next two notes.

Once you understand these two principles you should not have any trouble playing the arrangement.

Moderately

accel.   poco   a   poco

Brightly

INTERMEZZO
(A LOVE STORY)

ROBERT HENNING
HEINZ PROVOST

Before beginning to play this arrangement, tune your E or sixth string down to D. The D should be one octave lower than the D or fourth string. The first chord of the second measure should be played with a 1/2 bar at the second fret.

At measure 13, set the bar at the sixth fret on the third note of the measure. This will prepare you for the rest of the measure.

To play measure 19, keep a 1/2 bar at the fifth fret for the entire measure. The same thing applies to measure 25 at the seventh fret.

At measure 31, the E is to be slurred to D on the fifth string. This is a hard slur to play and will take extra practice.

The right hand fingering is very important in the animato section beginning on measure 33. In this measure, your "a" finger hits the high B and your thumb, "p", hits the low G and moves to the open D, or fourth string. "I" and "m" follow on the next notes. In order to bring out a good strong melody line in this section, your "a" finger should use the apoyando stroke.

The wavy line before the chords in measure 38 indicates that the chord should be played with a downward motion of the thumb.

Harmonics are called for in measure 52. Place your fourth finger on the first, second and third strings, directly *above* the 12th fret. Don't push down on the strings. Hit the three notes with "p," "i," "m" and the harmonic chord will be the result.

The same principle is applied to the harmonic called for in measure 53. Place your third finger directly above the 12th fret on the fifth string and strike the string with your thumb.

SH 4839
Used by permission

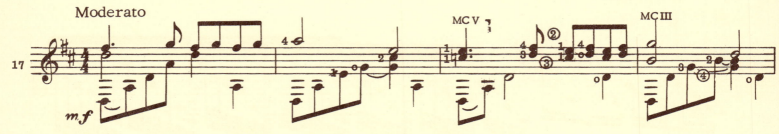

Moderato

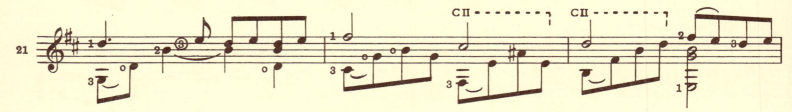

Animato

17

SH 4839

Theme of the M-G-M Picture "GREEN DOLPHIN STREET"

ON GREEN DOLPHIN STREET

NED WASHINGTON
BRONISLAU KAPER

Begin playing this arrangement with a bar at the fifth fret. The position remains through the next measure. To keep the tied E in measure 2 sounding, play it on the first open string and the next E is played closed on the second string.

In measure 18 you must use a 3/4 bar at the second fret leaving the fifth string open so that the A can be sounded.

Measure 19 introduces triplets which are then used throughout the arrangement. A triplet is a group of three notes played in the time value of two. This rhythmic device is vitally important to this arrangement.

To play measure 42 easily, use your fourth finger on the last note, C♯ of measure 41, and then slide it up to E on the second string and right into your bar.

Finally, be sure to play the second half of measure 44 and measure 45 with a bar at the ninth fret.

SH 4839

Rubato

Theme from the French Cafe Scene in the 20th Century-Fox Picture "THE RAZOR'S EDGE"

MAM'SELLE

MACK GORDON
EDMUND GOULDING

Before beginning to play this arrangement, be sure to tune the sixth string down one whole tone from E to D.

Use a half-barre at the second fret on the fourth beat of the first full measure. Also, use a half-barre at the fifth fret at measure 8.

The best way to play measure 12 is to use a half-barre at the second fret and keep it in place for the entire measure. The same thing applies for measure 14.

To play the harmonic at measure 19, place your third finger just above the seventh fret on the fourth string. Do not push down on the string. Then strike the string lightly with your finger and a harmonic sound will be the result.

There is a difficult stretch for your third and fourth fingers on the first beat of measure 26. Practice the chord several times by itself before continuing to play the rest of this arrangement.

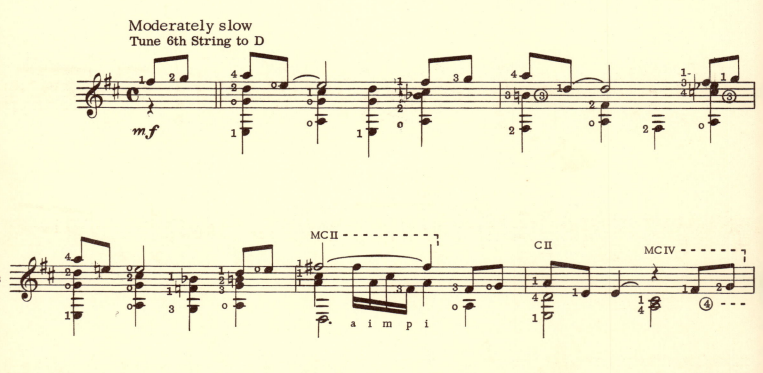

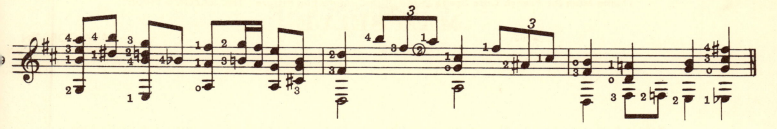

EBB TIDE

CARL SIGMAN
ROBERT MAXWELL

Once you have the chord set in place for the first measure, don't move it. The second and third measures are exactly the same, with only the first finger moving from C to D and back to C again. Watch the right hand fingering carefully to be sure you are alternating properly.

To keep the B ringing in measure 5, finger the open B string first. The second B appears as part of the arpeggio and should be fingered closed on the third string. This same device is used throughout the arrangement and sometimes creates tricky left hand fingerings that will take extra practice.

In measures 10 and 18 be sure to bar the fifth fret on the last beat of the measure.

The triplet in measure 21 is played by moving the first finger from A to B and back to A. Remember, the triplet is given the same amount of time as two eighth notes:

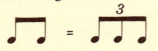

There is long reach in measure 31 that may cause some trouble, so watch your fingering. The lowest note, A is played on the sixth string and the high C is on the first string.

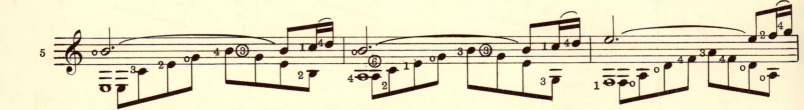

rit.   a tempo

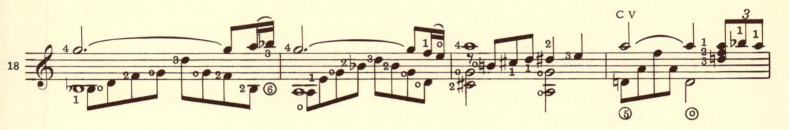

rit.   a tempo

rit.

Metro-Goldwyn-Mayer presents David Lean's Film "DOCTOR ZHIVAGO"

SOMEWHERE, MY LOVE

PAUL FRANCIS WEBSTER
MAURICE JARRE

Much of this arrangement consists of a series of eighth note triplets. The timing is: [♪♪♪]³ = ♩♩. If you begin with a bar at the fifth fret, you are in position to play the thirds at the eighth and ninth positions.

Measure 5 is best played with a 1/2 bar at the second fret.

Be especially careful in measure 8 to finger the left hand exactly as it is marked. Your third finger should be on the high B, so that your fourth finger can be free to hit the G on the second string. Then you move to a bar at the eighth position and end the musical phrase with a 1/2 bar at the ninth fret.

The wavy line in front of the chords in measures 13 and 15 means that the chord is to be hit with a downward motion of the thumb. The same symbol is used to indicate that the notes should be slightly arpeggiated rather than played at the same time.

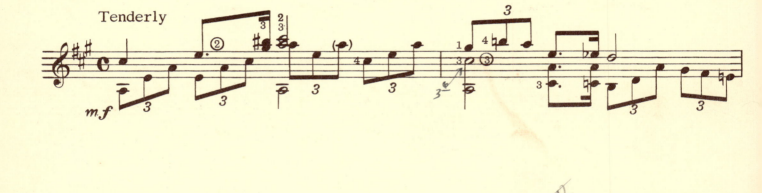

SH 4839

Appassionadamente

rit. e dim.

Theme Melody of the 20th Century-Fox Picture "LAURA"

LAURA

JOHNNY MERCER
DAVID RAKSIN

The first thing to do before playing this arrangement is to tune your E or sixth string down to D. It should be one octave lower than the D or fourth string.

In measure 6, play all the middle notes under a bar at the third fret. The bar can then slide to the second fret for the next measure.

To play the tremolo effect in measure 18, hold the fingers of the right hand close to the first string. Strike the B first with the "a" finger, followed quickly by "m" and "i." Your thumb strikes the bass note (in this case an A) at the same time a is striking the first note of the tremolo. While this pattern [$^{a,m,i}_{p}$] is being repeated, try not to move your hand any more than necessary.

After the tremolo section, be careful to read the notes in the proper positions. For instance, the thirds in measure 23 are played on the second and third strings.

Regarding the triplets beginning on measure 30: be careful of the rhythm here. The triplets take up the entire second and fourth beats of the measure: (♩♩♩ = ♩)

The trill indicated in the cadenza, measure 37, is played by doing a very fast slur from F to G♭ on the sixth string. It is best to do this with your first and second fingers.

The grace notes in the following measure are done by making a quick descending slur from the grace note to the regular note. This series should gradually build in volume until the final A♯ is reached.

SH 4839

SH 4839

Slowly, a tempo

Cadenza

a piacere

ten.

molto rit.

Piu mosso

ten.

Poco meno mosso

MC IV

espressivo

STAIRWAY TO THE STARS
Melody based on a Theme from "PARK AVENUE FANTASY"

MITCHELL PARISH
MATT MALNECK
FRANK SIGNORELLI

The introduction to this arrangement is quite effective and can be easily played by setting the chord, as fingered, with a half barre at the XIth fret. Lightly brush across the strings with your "i" finger, from the highest to the lowest, then brush back from the lowest to the highest. In the third measure, the chord slides to a half barre at the IXth fret where the same process is repeated.

Play the second half of measure 8 with a half barre at the IInd fret. Also, at measure 15, the third beat should be played with a half barre at the VIth fret.

There is a difficult "five fret" reach in measure 16, so be careful and practice it several times to be sure that you have the correct notes.

At measure 25, the rhythm might look complicated, but the way the voices are arranged you actually play on each eighth note beat; in other words, play 1 & 2 & 3 & 4 &, as if they were all eighth notes.

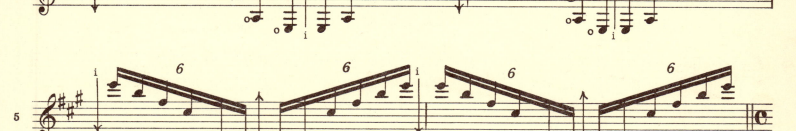

30

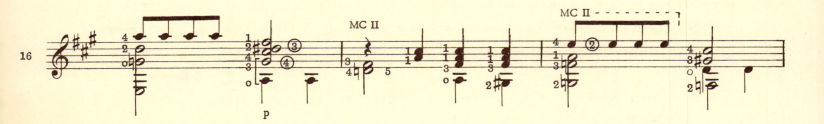

SH 4839

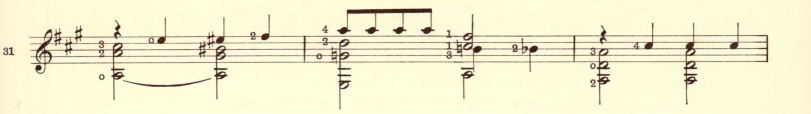

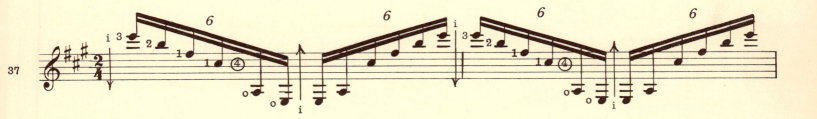

Metro-Goldwyn-Mayer and Filmways Present A Martin Ransohoff Production "THE SANDPIPER"

THE SHADOW OF YOUR SMILE
(LOVE THEME FROM "THE SANDPIPER")

PAUL FRANCIS WEBSTER
JOHNNY MANDEL

The beginning of this arrangement moves around quite a bit, so be careful that you are reading the chords on the proper strings and in the proper positions. For instance, the first measure is in the first position, the second measure moves to the third position, and then the third measure moves to a bar in the fifth position.

Measure 17 is played in the seventh position with the E played on the third string; the F♯ and G on the second string and the high B on the first string.

Measure 26 introduces a bar problem. Play a one-half bar with the fourth finger of your left hand. This may prove difficult the first few times, but it should become easier with more practice. The same thing occurs in measure 40, where the one-half bar is in the seventh position instead of the second position.

SH 4839

STAR EYES

DON RAYE and
GENE dePAUL

This arrangement has some tricky spots, but with practice can be very smooth and beautiful.

First of all, be sure to keep the bar at the second fret from the first to the second measure, as it is marked. The same passage is repeated several times through the song.

There is a difficult part beginning on the third beat of measure 5. Play the third beat chord on the appropriate strings (②③⑤) as it is marked. Then on the second half of the fourth beat your second finger slides up to the XIth fret. On the second beat of measure 6, the first finger will move to hit both the D♮ and then C♯, and will be right in position to move into a CIX. The same thing is found in measures 14, 15 and 30, 31.

At measure 12, on the second half of the third beat, the A is played with the second finger which then slides right into a half-barre at the sixth fret.

Measure 36 and 37 has a quick sixteenth-note phrase on the last beat which requires movement: first, from the IXth to the VIIth position, and second, from the IVth to the II position. This should be practiced several times.

The last chord requires a very difficult reach. The hardest part is to keep the high F♯ sounding while you are stretching to G♯ with your 4th finger. As with any difficult stretch, extra practice should solve the problem.

Laurindo Almeida with Joey Bishop   *...with Mike Douglas*

SOFTLY, AS I LEAVE YOU
(PIANO)

G. CALABRESE
HAL SHAPER
A. DE VITA

The entire introduction of this arrangement is played using harmonics instead of regular notes. To play the harmonics, place your 4th finger lightly on the appropriate string, just above the fret. For the first A, put your 4th finger on the fifth string at the XII fret. Then strike the string and the result should be a harmonic. If it is not, it is very likely that your finger is not directly above the fret. Keep experimenting until the right spot is found. Also, remember that a circled number is the number of the string.

In measure 6, the F in the chord on the second beat is a tied note and is therefore not played. Only hit the upper two notes: A and D of the chord.

To play the second half of measure 16, it is necessary to move first finger from B♭ to A♭ as part of the arpeggio. The first finger should not be used as a barre in this case.

There is a rather difficult reach starting on the third beat of measure 26, so be careful that your fingers are properly placed. Your second finger is on E on the fifth string and your first finger is on C on the third string.

Another big stretch is found in measure 27. The fourth finger must stay on C at the VIII fret for the entire measure. Then the third finger moves from A♭ to E♭ within the arpeggio.

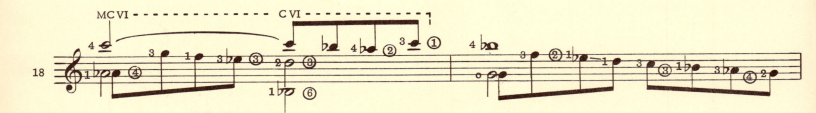

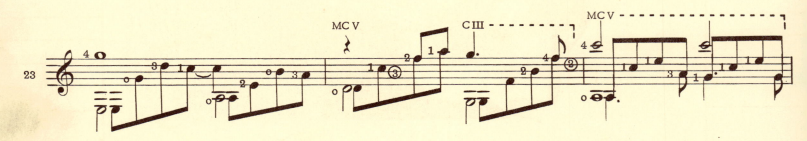

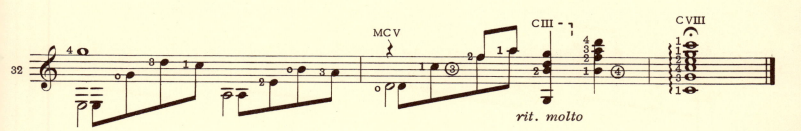

rit. molto

From the MGM Picture "LILI"

HI-LILI, HI-LO

HELEN DEUTSCH
BRONISLAU KAPER

The little grace notes beginning on measure 13 are played a little differently in this arrangement than they were in "Zorba." Instead of slurring from one note to another on the same string, the slur, this time, is played by quickly going from A♯ on the third string to the open B string. The best right hand fingering for this measure (13) is to have "p" and "a" hit the first two notes together, and then let "i," "m" take care of the slur. This same right hand pattern can be repeated throughout this section.

Some extra pointers about left hand fingering: measure four should be played with a bar at the second fret. Remember that ⑥ means the sixth string, so in measure 18 play the B on the sixth string at the seventh fret.

The harmonic effect required for the last note in this arrangement is achieved by placing your fourth finger on the string directly *above* the twelfth fret. Do not push down on the string. Strike the string with your "i" finger. This results in a harmonic.

Theme of the M-G-M Film
THE BAD AND THE BEAUTIFUL

The Bad And The Beautiful is by far the most difficult arrangement in this collection. It might be helpful to listen to Laurindo Almeida's recording of "The Bad And The Beautiful" (Capitol Album Number P-8447) as you are learning to play it. The following describes some of the trouble spots that you will encounter.

In the first measure, on the second beat, bar the IIIrd fret and hold it through the second and third beats. This is a difficult reach for the 4th finger since it must hit the A♭ and then move to A♮.

Be sure to play the first C♮ in the second measure on the third string, as it is marked, so that you will be in position for the barre IV which follows on the next beat.

Arpeggiate the first chord in measure 4. This chord is played with a bar at the IXth fret, but remember to leave the sixth string open. The same thing applies for the first chord in measure 5.

The fourth beat of measure 5 is a difficult chord because you must bar the VIIth fret and reach to put your 2nd finger on B on the sixth string while at the same time playing the high D with the 4th finger on the first string. Getting from this to the chord progression in measure 6 will take extra practice.

The chord progression in measure 6 begins with a five fret stretch from the Xth fret to the XIVth fret, Then slide your 4th finger back to D on the second beat. Bar the IXth fret on the third beat and just slide the same bar to the VIIth fret, keeping the 3rd finger in place and lifting the 2nd finger, which will hit the G on the last half of the fourth beat.

The time changes to $\frac{3}{4}$ in measure 10. The first chord is another five fret reach, with your 4th finger on A, 3rd finger on D, 2nd finger on F♮ and your 1st finger on B♭.

In measure 15, you must move from the IXth fret to a bar at the IInd fret, and another long reach. The 3rd finger must play the last D while the bar is held down.

Practice the chord progressions in measures 16, 17 and 18 many times to be sure that you are playing the correct accidentals. There are many added flats that may sound a little strange at first, but once you put it all together it actually sounds quite beautiful.

To play measure 20, slide your 4th finger from G at the IIIrd fret to D at the Xth fret and continue playing the bass line as it is marked, on the fifth string.

To prepare for the second beat of measure 21, slide your first finger from E to F♯ and then into a five string bar at the IXth fret. The same thing happens in measure 25 from the IInd to the IVth frets. Remember to arpeggiate the chords as marked.

Use a bar at the IXth fret on the last beat of measure 31.

The last difficult reach is found on the third beat of measure 33. Your 3rd finger is on A, 4th finger on F♯, 1st finger on B♭ and the 2nd finger on C♯.

Theme of the M-G-M Film

THE BAD AND THE BEAUTIFUL

DORY LANGDON
DAVID RAKSIN

Slowly
Tune 6th String to D

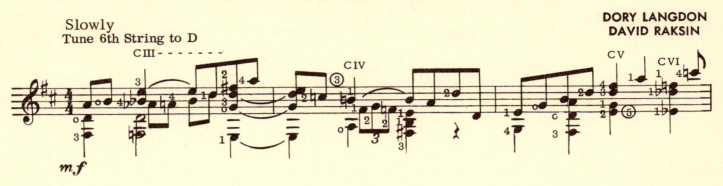

SH 4839

44

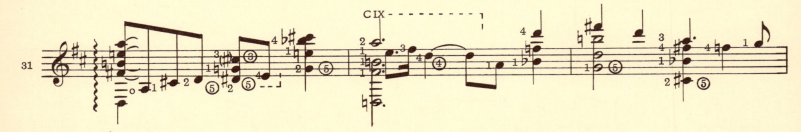

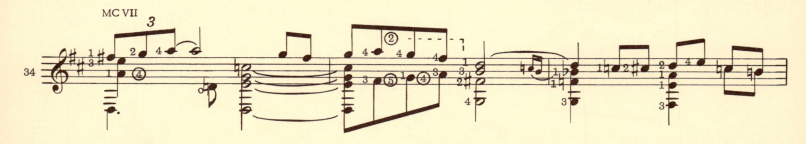

SH 4839

From the Metro-Goldwyn-Mayer Motion Picture "MEET ME IN ST. LOUIS"

THE BOY NEXT DOOR

HUGH MARTIN
RALPH BLANE

Be sure to set your barre VI in position on the last beat of the first measure, so that you will be ready to play the second measure. This same pattern appears again, beginning on the last beat of the third measure, except this time the barre is at the IV fret.

When bass notes are connected by a bracket, as in measure 7, they are played together with a single stroke of the thumb. Of course to achieve this, the higher A will have to be played on the fourth string at the VII fret, so the two notes will be on adjacent strings.

In measure 11, B on the third string is slurred to C, also on the third string. To execute this slur, the 4th finger must slide from the B to the C. This is difficult and may require extra practice.

There is a tricky change for your 4th finger in measure 14, so be careful to play it just as it is fingered.

In the section beginning on measure 35, play the thirds on the first beat with the E closed on the second string. Use your 3rd and 4th fingers as indicated; then the next third, D and B, should be played with the 1st and 2nd fingers. In this way you can stay within the third position for the entire measure. The pattern is repeated throughout this section and should be played the same way each time.

46

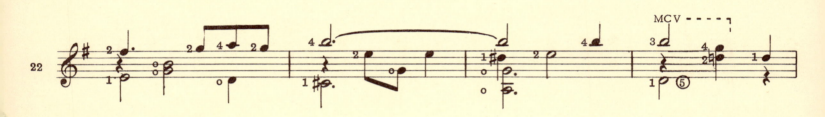

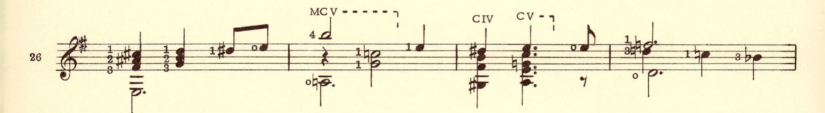

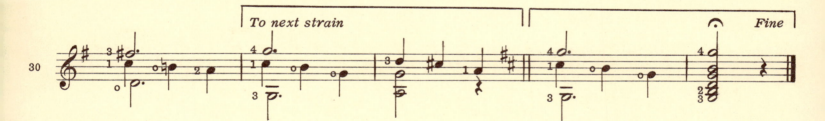

SH 4839

D.C. al Fine

Based on the Theme of the M-G-M Picture "INVITATION"

INVITATION

PAUL FRANCIS WEBSTER
BRONISLAU KAPER

This arrangement begins with a bar at the fifth fret. The fourth finger must first stretch to hit the lower B and then move to the first string to play the high B.

Once again a triplet rhythm is dominant throughout the piece. This time the rhythm is: ♩♩♩ = ♩♩.

At measure 21, bar the second fret and play the G♯ with your fourth finger. Then slide the fourth finger to A♯ and bar the fourth fret.

Measures 23, 24 and 25 can all be played with a bar at the second fret. In measure 23, play the upper G♯ with the fourth finger while the third finger plays the lower C♯. Keep the third finger on C♯ for the next measure and move the fourth finger to F♯ on the fourth string.

The last measure is played with a bar at the first fret and the fourth finger hitting the B closed on the third string.

MIMI

LAURINDO ALMEIDA

Mimi is an original song by Laurindo Almeida and the only Bossa Nova piece in this collection, so it is necessary to say a word about the rhythm. The most frequently found rhythm is as follows:

Broken down to eighth notes

or, as it appears

Practice this rhythm several times before getting into the music, just to get the feel of the Bossa beat.

In measure 14, use a half-barre X for the first chord and merely move it one fret lower to half-barre IX for the second chord.

The easiest way to play measure 15 is to keep a barre at VII fret for the entire measure.

Barre the VII fret on the third beat of measure 22 and keep the barre for the rest of the measure. In this way your first finger is right in position for the B on the last beat of the measure.

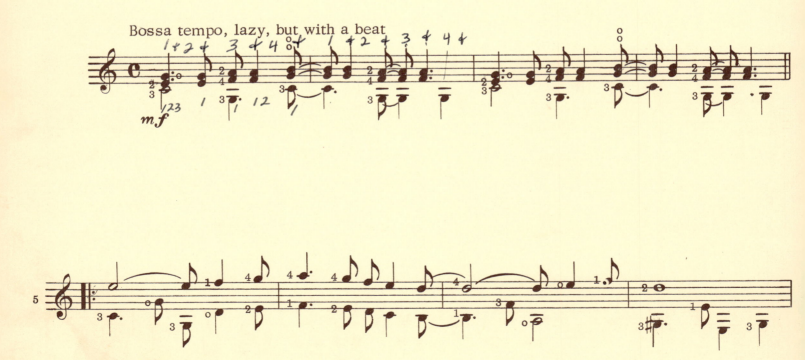

From the M-G-M Picture "THE WIZARD OF OZ"

OVER THE RAINBOW

E. Y. HARBURG
HAROLD ARLEN

The harmonics in the first measure are executed by placing the 4th finger directly over the XII fret of the first and second strings and striking them lightly with your thumb, "p," and "i" finger. Do the same thing in the second measure at the VII fret.

In measure 7, the E in the first chord is to be slurred to D. This is done with the 3rd finger and may cause some difficulty, so practice it several times.

The first chord in measure 18 requires a five fret reach with the 1st finger on C♯, the 2nd finger stretching two frets to B, and the 4th finger on G♯. It is always easier to make an extra stretch between the 1st and 2nd fingers than between the 3rd and 4th fingers. This is the reason for this fingering.

The marking "✗" indicates a double sharp. In other words, sharp the sharp. So in measure 22, F✗ is the same as G.

SH 4839

DEEP PURPLE

MITCHELL PARISH
PETER DE ROSE

The best way to play the chord progression in measure 9 is to keep a half-barre at the VIII fret for the entire measure. In this way, the barre will be on the third beat where it is needed. The same kind of pattern should be used in the next two measures. Set your position at the beginning of the measure and let it remain there until the end. Only the upper voice line moves.

In measure 14, slide the thirds from the V fret to the XI fret as the fingering indicates.

Watch for the movement in measure 19. Remember that a circled number indicates the string on which a note is to be played. The notes are right under the fingers between the VIII and XII frets.

Measure 26 has a very long stretch that may require extra practice. You must have your 1st finger on C, 2nd finger on E♭ and your 4th finger on high B.

The chord on the first beat of measure 31 is executed by playing the two lower notes, in brackets, with your thumb (p), and striking the upper three notes with your fingers. The wavy line in front of the chord means that the chord should be arpeggiated or rolled.

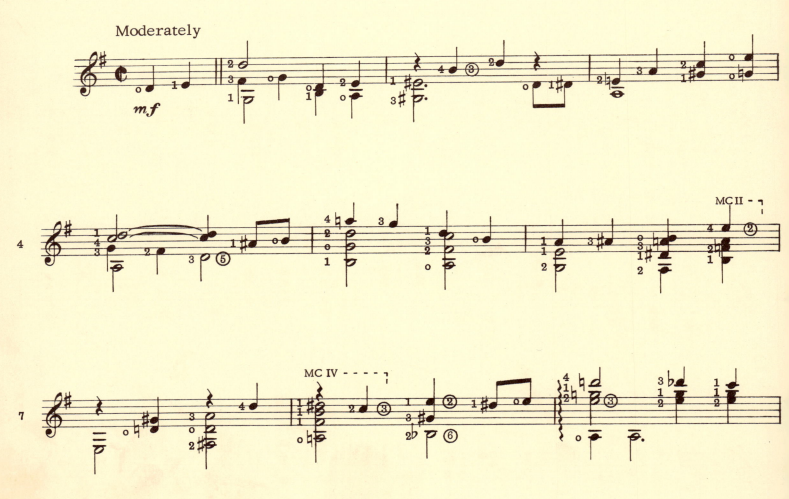

SH 4839   International Copyright Secured   Made in U.S.A.   All Rights Reserved

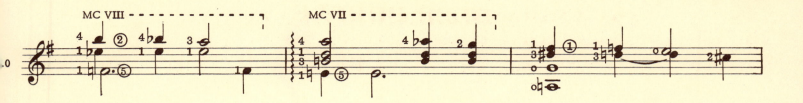

SH 4839

I'M ALWAYS CHASING RAINBOWS

JOSEPH McCARTHY
HARRY CARROLL

In measure 2, slide your fourth finger from G♯ up to high B. You are now in position for the barre IV.

The first trouble spot in this arrangement occurs in measure 5 on the third beat. Here your 1st finger must do all the shifting in order to play the three notes as they are marked. Also, be careful that your 2nd finger hits the E♯ on the proper string. It is sometimes difficult to hit the right note when strings are skipped, so be sure that your fingers are placed correctly.

Hold barre II from measure 6 halfway through measure 7 as marked.

In measure 8, the x indicates a double sharp. In other words, sharp the sharp. In this case C x = D.

SH 4839   International Copyright Secured   Made in U.S.A.   All Rights Reserved

From the Batjac Production "THE ALAMO". A United Artists Release

THE GREEN LEAVES OF SUMMER

PAUL FRANCIS WEBSTER
DIMITRI TIOMKIN

This arrangement consists almost entirely of arpeggios. To continue to play the melody, it becomes necessary to move your fingers within the arpeggio. The first example of this occurs in measure 6, where you must take your finger off the D♯ on the fourth beat, so that the B will be open for the chord.

Also in measure 6, the wavy line in front of the chord indicates it should be arpeggiated. In other words, all the notes are not hit at the same time.

On the fourth beat of measure 13, slide your first finger from B on the fourth string to G♯ also on the fourth string. The first finger slides the same way in measure 15.

The easiest way to play measure 18 is to slide the second and third fingers from the II to the Vth fret, just as it is marked.

Play the harmonics in the last measure by placing the fourth finger on the first three strings just above the 12th fret. Then hit the strings with "p," "i" and "m."

Moderately

SPRING IS HERE

(Featured in Dwight Deere Wiman's Musical Comedy "I MARRIED AN ANGEL")

LORENZ HART
RICHARD RODGERS

Make sure that your middle barre in measure two only covers three strings, because the D must be left open when it is hit on the third beat. The same kind of barre situation occurs in measure 3.

Also in measure 3, you will find a triplet. That is, three notes played in the same time span as two:

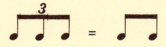

The chord progressions beginning on measures 9 and 13 are very beautiful and move from the first position to the seventh position. Be careful to hit the notes on the strings as marked. Remember, a circled number indicates the number of the string on which the note is to be played.

The wavy line in front of the chord in measure 12 means that the chord should be arpeggiated or rolled. In other words, strike all the notes of the chord quickly in succession from the bottom to the top.

In measure 16, bar the V fret for the entire second half of the measure.

SH 4839

Theme Melody of the 20th Century-Fox CinemaScope Production "ANASTASIA"

ANASTASIA

PAUL FRANCIS WEBSTER
ALFRED NEWMAN

Be sure to keep a half-barre at the II fret for the first four measures of this arrangement. The reach for the 3rd and 4th fingers is a full four frets, so a little extra practice may be necessary.

Another long reach is found in measure 25. Here the 3rd finger plays the low G♯ and must remain there while the 2nd and 4th fingers play D and B.

The harmonic in measure 26 is made at the XII fret on the sixth string. Hold your 4th finger just *above* the fret and strike the string with your thumb. Another harmonic occurs in measure 36 and should be played using the same method on the first string at the XII fret.

In measure 33, be sure to hit the A on the first beat with your 3rd finger, as marked, so that you don't run out of fingers for the rest of the measure.

H. 12